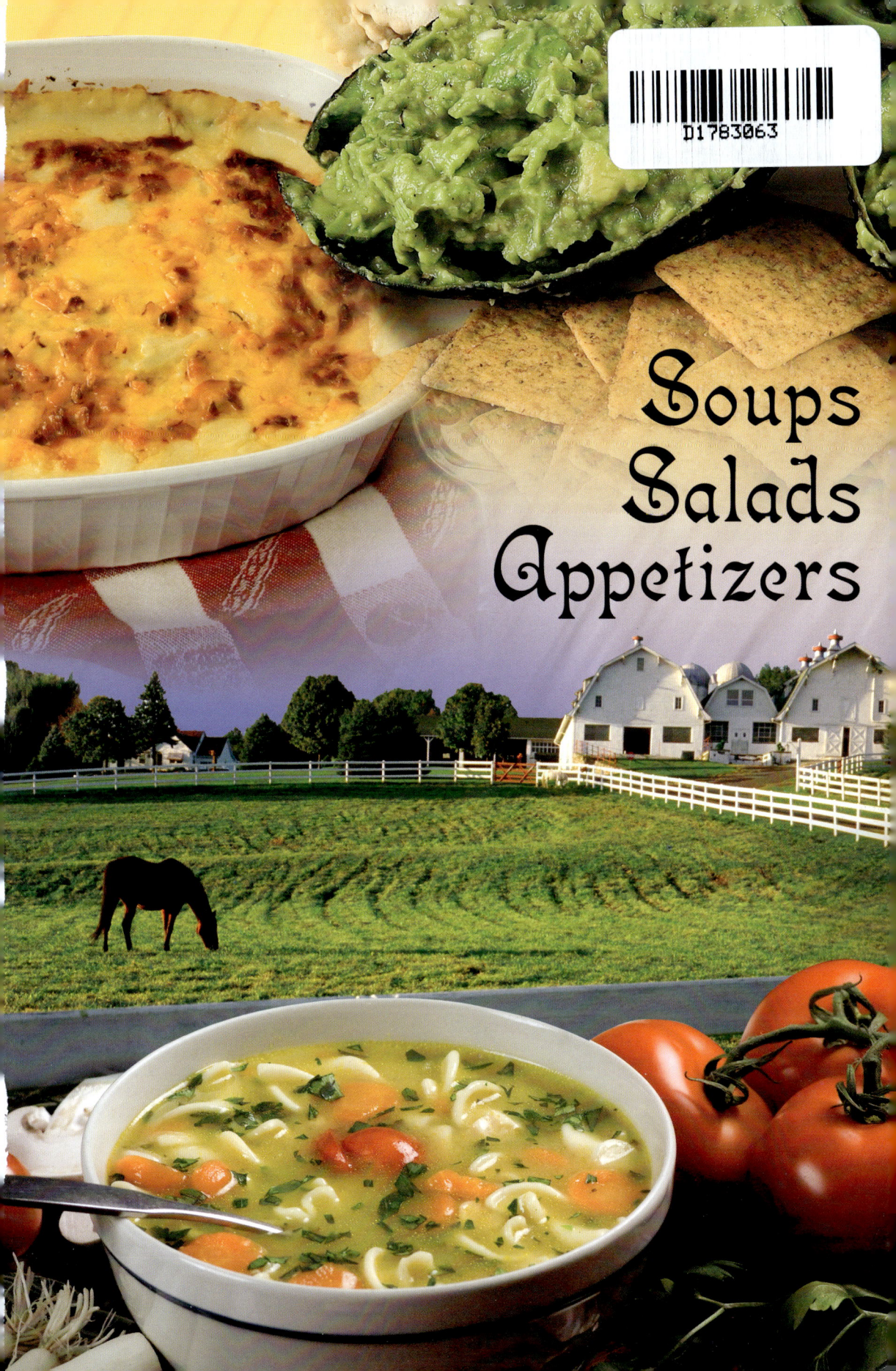

Soups
Salads
Appetizers

Vegetable Soup

5	cups beef broth	1/2	cup each of a combination of the following ingredients:
2	15-ounce cans crushed tomatoes		corn, green beans, celery, peas,
1/2	pound cubed chuck roast		carrots, potatoes, turnips
1	onion, finely chopped		

Sauté the onion in a small amount of oil until translucent. Add the meat and brown. Add the broth and tomatoes. Cook on low heat for 30 minutes. Add the chopped vegetables and cook an additional 15-20 minutes. Season with salt and pepper.

Lentil Soup

(A stored food favorite) Brown lentils hold their shape and are used in salads. Red or orange lentils cook to a soft, mushy consistency and are used as a side dish or in soups.

1	pound dried lentil beans	1	garlic clove, minced
1	ham hock	1	teaspoon salt
4	cups beef broth		Pepper to taste
1	medium onion, diced	1	ring of wurst or 1/2 pound wieners, cut in bite size (optional)
2	stalks celery, chopped		
1	carrot, chopped		

Place lentils in a stockpot with ham bone and broth. Add water, if needed, to cover beans. Cover pot and simmer 15 minutes. Add remaining ingredients. Simmer covered for 1 hour. Add wieners or wurst 10 minutes before serving. Serves 6.

Chicken Noodle Soup

1	3-pound broiler/fryer chicken	1	small onion, chopped
1-1/2	teaspoons salt	1	carrot, pared and diced
	water to cover chicken	1	celery stalk, thinly sliced
1-1/2	cups fine noodles	1	bay leaf
			additional salt and pepper to taste

Wash chicken, remove innards but do not cut up. Cover chicken with water in large pot. Add salt. Heat to boiling. Reduce heat; cover and simmer 1-1/2 hours or until chicken is tender.

Remove chicken from broth. Remove meat from bones and cut into small pieces. Skim fat from broth. Measure broth into medium saucepan (add water if necessary to have 5 cups). Add chicken meat and remaining ingredients. Heat to boiling. Reduce heat and simmer until noodles are tender, about 15 minutes. Remove bay leaf before serving. Makes 6 servings.

Appetizers, Soups & Salads

Potato Cheese Chowder

6	medium potatoes, peeled and cubed	3	cups milk
2	medium onions, finely chopped	3	tablespoons butter
4	stalks celery, finely chopped	3	tablespoons flour
4	carrots, diced	1	tablespoon dry mustard
4	cups chicken broth (or water)		Salt and pepper to taste
1	10-ounce package frozen broccoli	12	ounces American cheese, cubed

Cook potatoes, onions, celery and carrots in broth or water until tender, about 30 minutes. Add broccoli and milk. In skillet, melt butter and add flour and dry mustard to make a roux (a mixture of fat and flour used to thicken sauces). Stir roux into soup until thickened. Add cheese and stir until melted. Simmer until ready to serve. Serves 8.

Fresh Cream of Tomato Soup

4	cups tomatoes, chopped	1	bay leaf
1	medium onion, chopped	1	teaspoon salt
4	sprigs parsley, minced	1	teaspoon sugar
6	whole cloves	2	cups thin white sauce (recipe follows)
1/2	teaspoon dried basil, crumbled		

Simmer tomatoes and all ingredients, except white sauce, about ten minutes until tomatoes are mushy. Rub tomato mixture through a sieve or process in a blender. Add boiling water, if necessary, to reach 2 cups purée. Pour slowly into hot thin white sauce. Stir well and serve. Yields 4 servings

White Sauce (thin)

3 tablespoons butter	2 tablespoons flour
1 teaspoon salt	1/4 teaspoon white pepper
2 cups milk	

Melt butter over low heat; add flour, salt, and pepper. Stir until well blended. Remove from heat. Gradually stir in milk and return to heat, stirring constantly until thick and smooth.

Mormon Family Recipes

Emerald Salad
(A stored food favorite)

1	package (3 ounces) lemon flavored gelatin	1	cup mayonnaise
1	package (3 ounces) lime flavored gelatin	1	cup cottage cheese, drained
		1	cup evaporated milk
2	cups liquid, heated (pineapple juice plus water)	1	cup nuts, chopped
		1	cup crushed pineapple, drained

Dissolve gelatins in hot liquid. Chill until partially set. Whip with electric mixer until fluffy. Blend in remaining ingredients. Pour into an 8-cup mold or individual molds. Chill until set. Often molded in a ring and served with the center filled with fruit cocktail. Makes 10 servings.

Green Goddess Salad
(A traditional fancy favorite)

1	clove garlic, minced	3	tablespoons tarragon-wine vinegar
1/2	teaspoon salt	1	cup mayonnaise
1/2	teaspoon dry mustard	1/2	cup commercial sour cream
1	teaspoon Worcestershire sauce	4	cups crisp mixed salad greens in bite-size pieces
2	tablespoons anchovy paste	1	cup cooked shrimp or crab meat (optional)
3	tablespoons snipped parsley	2	tomatoes, quartered
1/8	teaspoon black pepper		

Combine all seasonings thoroughly with vinegar, mayonnaise and sour cream. Add about 1/3 of this dressing to salad greens and shrimp (or crab), tossing gently. Garnish with tomato wedges; serve at once. (Refrigerate remaining dressing. It will keep well for several days.) Makes 4 servings.

Mixed Bean Salad and Cider Vinegar Dressing

1/4	cup cider vinegar	1/4	teaspoon pepper
1/4	cup sugar	1/3	cup vegetable oil
1/2	teaspoon salt		

Whisk together vinegar, sugar, salt and pepper in a large bowl. Add oil in a thin, slow stream, whisking until thoroughly combined. Prepare salad.

1	15-ounce can of each: French style green beans cut green beans yellow wax beans red kidney beans	1	cup red onion, finely chopped
		1	cup sweet red pepper, finely chopped
		1/2	cup celery, finely chopped
		1/4	cup parsley, finely chopped

Drain liquid from beans. Rinse beans in cold water and drain. Add all ingredients to dressing; toss to mix. Cover and refrigerate 2 hours or overnight. Serves 8 to 10.

"Prepare ye, prepare ye for that which is to come."
...Doctrine and Covenants, Section 1, Verse 12

"If any provide not for his own, and specially for those of his own house, he hath denied the faith." .....1 Timothy 5:8

Summer Salad

1	3-ounce package peach-flavored gelatin	1/4	cup diced honeydew melon
1	cup boiling water	1/2	cup blueberries, rinsed and drained
3/4	cup cold water	1/4	cup seedless grapes, sliced
1	cup ripe peaches, sliced		lettuce leafs

Dissolve gelatin in boiling water. Mix in cold water. Refrigerate until mixture begins to thicken. Blend in fruit gently, distributing it throughout gelatin mixture. Refrigerate several hours, or overnight, until firm. Serve on lettuce leaves. Makes 6 servings.

Potato Salad

3	cups cooked and cooled diced potatoes	1	tablespoon prepared yellow mustard
2/3	cup diced celery	3	tablespoons sour cream
1/2	cup green onions and tops, thinly sliced	1	tablespoon vinegar
1/4	cup pimiento, chopped	1	teaspoon dried dill
1/3	cup sweet Gherkin pickles, chopped	3/4	teaspoon salt
4	eggs, hard-boiled, cooled and chopped	1/4	teaspoon pepper
2/3	cup mayonnaise or salad dressing		Paprika

Combine the first 6 ingredients in a large bowl. In a separate bowl, combine the remaining ingredients. Gently mix into the potato mixture. Refrigerate, covered for at least 2 hours. Makes 6 servings.

Mormon Family Recipes

Pigs in a Blanket

1 package hot dogs or sausage links   1 can crescent roll dough

Preheat oven 400°. Separate dough into triangles. Roll up links in dough, starting with the link at the wide end of the triangle. Place on ungreased baking sheet, with the tip of the crescent underneath (or it will come undone a bit as the dough rises in baking). Bake for 10-15 minutes or until golden brown. Cut into bite size pieces. Makes 24

Chile-Cheese Log

3/4	pound natural Cheddar cheese, grated	1/8	teaspoon garlic salt
1	3-ounce package cream cheese, softened	1-1/2	teaspoons Worcestershire sauce
1/4	teaspoon salt		Chili powder
1/8	teaspoon pepper		

Several days ahead, combine Cheddar and cream cheeses thoroughly with seasonings. Shape into 2 thin logs. Sprinkle waxed paper with chili powder and roll each cheese log until coated with chili powder. Wrap logs in waxed paper; refrigerate for 3 or 4 days to ripen. To serve, arrange logs on board for slicing with assorted crackers nearby. Makes about 1 pound.

Salsa Mushrooms

12	large fresh white mushrooms	1/2	cup crushed tortilla chips
	vegetable oil	1/2	cup grated Monterey Jack cheese
1/2	cup fresh or prepared tomato salsa		

Preheat oven to 350 degrees. Remove mushroom stems; discard or save for another use. Brush both sides of mushroom caps with oil. Place mushrooms, hollow side up, in a single layer on an oiled baking sheet. Stir together salsa and crushed chips. Fill caps with mixture and sprinkle with cheese. Bake until mushrooms are warm and cheese is melted, about 15 minutes. Serve immediately. Makes 12 servings.

Guacamole in Shell

2	large ripe avocados	1	tablespoon minced onion
2	tablespoons lemon juice	1	medium tomato, seeded, drained and chopped
1/2	teaspoon salt	1/2	cup commercial sour cream
2	green chili peppers, finely chopped		

Cut avocados in half lengthwise; remove pits. With a teaspoon, scoop out pulp, keeping shells intact. Sprinkle inside of avocado shells with half of lemon juice. Mash avocado pulp with remaining lemon juice and other ingredients. Return mixture to avocado shells and serve as a dip for crackers, chips, shrimp or vegetables. Serves 6 to 8.

Spicy Meat Balls

1/2	pound ground beef	1/4	teaspoon nutmeg
1	egg	1/4	teaspoon liquid hot pepper seasoning
1/2	cup dry bread crumbs		
2	teaspoons minced onion	2	tablespoons salad oil
1/2	teaspoon salt		Blue cheese dipping sauce (recipe follows)
1/4	teaspoon pepper		
1/4	teaspoon horseradish		

Combine beef with egg, crumbs, onion, and seasonings. Shape into one-inch balls; sauté in hot oil in large skillet until lightly browned on all sides. Serve on cocktail picks. Makes 3 dozen.

Blue Cheese Dipping Sauce

3	ounces crumbled blue cheese	1/2	teaspoon minced onion
1/2	pound cottage cheese	1/2	cup commercial sour cream

Combine all ingredients well. Serve in bowl for dipping.

Mormon Family Recipes

Sweet Potato Surprise
Children love to eat vegetables like this.

2	pounds yams or sweet potatoes	1/4	teaspoon salt
1/3	cup butter	12	large marshmallows
1/4	cup brown sugar	2	cups uncrushed cornflakes

Cook potatoes, covered, in small amount of boiling salted water until tender, about 30 minutes. Drain; peel and mash to make 4 cups. Season with butter, brown sugar and salt. Cool. With tablespoon, scoop up about 1/4 cup of mixture and press it around marshmallow. Add more as needed to cover marshmallow. Shape into balls and roll each ball in cornflakes. Place on buttered baking dish; cover with foil and refrigerate. When ready to cook, preheat oven to 325 degrees and bake 20 to 30 minutes. Makes 12 potato balls.

Green Bean Casserole
This is the original family favorite vegetable dish.

1	can (10-3/4 ounces) condensed cream of mushroom soup	2	packages (9 ounces each) frozen cut green beans, thawed and drained; or 2 cans (15 ounces each) cut green beans, drained
3/4	cup milk		
1/8	teaspoon ground black pepper	1-1/3	cups French's French Fried Onions, divided

Preheat oven to 350 degrees. Combine soup, milk and ground pepper in a 1-1/2-quart casserole; stir until well blended. Stir in beans and 2/3 cup French Fried Onions. Bake, uncovered, 30 minutes or until hot. Stir; spread top with remaining 2/3 cup onions. Bake 5 minutes or until onions are golden. Makes 6 servings.

Broccoli Cheese Bake

1	bunch broccoli (or 1 head cauliflower)	1/4	cup milk
1	can (10-3/4 ounces) condensed Cheddar cheese soup	2	tablespoons buttered bread crumbs
		6	slices bacon, cooked and crumbled

Trim flowerets from broccoli or cauliflower. Cut off coarse outer leaves and tough part of broccoli stalks. Peel stalks and cut into serving size pieces. Place in a saucepan and cover with one inch of water. Bring to a boil; cover tightly and cook 10 minutes, or until vegetables are barely tender. Drain; place in a shallow baking dish. Mix soup with milk and pour over vegetables. Top with crumbs. Bake at 350 degrees for 20 minutes. Garnish with bacon before serving. Serves 6.

Appetizers, Soups & Salads

Traditional Funeral Potatoes
There are many variations of this stored food favorite.

1-1/2	pounds frozen hash brown potatoes	3/4	cup milk
1	can (10-3/4 ounces) condensed cream of celery soup (or cream soup of choice)	1	cup sour cream
		1/2	cup grated cheese (American, Cheddar or Parmesan)
1	can (10-3/4 ounces) condensed cream of potato soup	2	tablespoons butter

Preheat oven to 350 degrees. Mix all ingredients except cheese and butter and pour into a shallow baking dish. Top with cheese and dot with butter. Bake for 1 hour or until cheese is melted and lightly browned. Makes 8 servings.

Creamed Spinach with Parmesan Cheese

1/2	teaspoon butter	1/2	teaspoon salt
2	packages (10 ounces each) frozen chopped spinach, drained	1/4	teaspoon freshly ground pepper
		1/4	teaspoon freshly grated nutmeg
1	cup heavy whipping cream	1/2	cup fresh bread crumbs
1/2	cup grated parmesan cheese		

Butter a shallow baking dish. Squeeze as much water as possible from the spinach. Place spinach and cream in a large saucepan and heat over medium high, stirring constantly. Reduce heat and stir in cheese to melt. Add salt, pepper and nutmeg. Adjust seasonings to taste. Transfer spinach mixture to baking dish and sprinkle with bread crumbs. When ready to serve, place dish in the oven a few inches below the broiler and broil until top is golden and crunchy, about 3 minutes. Makes 6 servings.

Ratatouille

1	medium eggplant	4	medium tomatoes, peeled and quartered
2	medium zucchini	1	clove garlic, crushed
2	tablespoons olive oil	2	teaspoons salt
1	cup finely chopped green pepper	1/4	teaspoon pepper
1	medium onion, finely chopped		

Cut eggplant into 1/2-inch cubes. Cut zucchini into 1/4-inch slices. Place in saucepan with oil and other ingredients. Stir to blend. Cover and cook over medium heat, stirring occasionally, about 10 minutes or until vegetables are crisp-tender. Makes 6 to 8 servings.

Glazed Carrots

2	pounds carrots	1	teaspoon grated orange peel
1/2	cup brown sugar	3	tablespoons butter
1/2	teaspoon salt		

Scrape carrots; cut off ends. Slice lengthwise into 1/2-inch-wide strips and cut crosswise in half. Place in saucepan with enough salted water to barely cover. Bring to a boil; cover and cook on medium until tender, about 20 minutes. In large skillet, cook and stir brown sugar and butter, add salt and orange peel, until bubbly, being careful not to burn. Add carrot strips; cook over low heat until carrots are glazed. Makes 6 servings.

Stuffed Peppers

4	red bell peppers	1 1/2	cups cooked rice
4	tablespoons extra-virgin olive oil	1	cup chopped tomatoes, fresh or canned
1	medium yellow onion, peeled and chopped	1	teaspoon of dried oregano
1	clove garlic, peeled and chopped	2/3	cup ketchup
1	lb of lean ground beef	1/2	teaspoon of Worcestershire Sauce

Bring a large pot of water to a boil over high heat. Meanwhile, cut top off peppers 1 inch from the stem end, and remove seeds. Add several generous pinches of salt to boiling water, then add peppers and boil, using a spoon to keep peppers completely submerged, until brilliant red and their flesh slightly softened, about 3 minutes. Drain, set aside to cool. Preheat oven to 350 degrees F. Heat 3 tbsp of the oil in a large skillet over medium heat. Add onions and garlic, and cook, stirring often, until soft and translucent, about 5 minutes. Remove skillet from heat, add meat, rice, tomatoes, and oregano, and season generously with salt and pepper. Mix well. Drizzle remaining 1 tbsp. oil inside peppers, arrange cut side up in a baking dish, and then stuff peppers with filling. Combine ketchup, a Worcestershire sauce, and 1/4 cup of water in a small bowl, then spoon over filling. Add 1/4 cup of water to the baking dish. Place in oven and bake for 30-40 minutes. Serves 4.

Chicken Skillet l`Orange

Delicious enough for the family to love but elegant enough for company.

1	broiler/fryer 3-pound chicken, cut up	1/2	teaspoon ground ginger
1/2	cup butter	1-1/2	cups orange juice
1/4	cup flour	1/1/2	cups water
1/2	teaspoon salt	1/2	teaspoon liquid hot pepper seasoning
1/2	teaspoon paprika	1	unpeeled orange
1/4	teaspoon pepper	1	can (18 ounces) vacuum-packed sweet potatoes
2	tablespoons brown sugar		

Sprinkle chicken with a little salt and paprika. Melt butter in large skillet, brown chicken on all sides. Lift chicken from skillet. In butter left in skillet (add more if necessary), stir flour, salt, pepper, sugar and ginger until thickened and smooth. Slowly stir in orange juice, water and liquid hot pepper seasoning. Cook, stirring until mixture thickens and comes to a boil. Add chicken; cover and simmer 30 minutes. Slice orange 1/2 inch thick and quarter slices. Add to chicken along with potatoes. Cover; simmer 15 more minutes or until chicken is tender. Serves 4.

Overnight Breakfast Casserole

8	slices white bread		8	slices Swiss cheese
1/4	cup butter		3	eggs
1	tablespoon prepared mustard		2	cups milk
8	slices cooked ham			

Spread the bread with a mixture of the butter and mustard. Put together with slices of ham and cheese. Cut each sandwich into 4 triangles. Line up sandwiches, pointed side up in a shallow 9" x 9" casserole dish. In a medium bowl, beat eggs with a whisk, add milk and mix well. Pour over the sandwiches, coating bread evenly. Cover dish with plastic wrap and refrigerate for at least 2 hours or overnight. Remove wrap and bake in a preheated 350-degree oven for 40 minutes or until puffed and golden. Serves 4-6

Classic Macaroni and Cheese
(A stored food favorite)

3	tablespoons butter, melted	3/4	pound elbow macaroni
3	tablespoons flour	1	teaspoon Worcestershire sauce
3	cups milk	10	ounces Sharp Cheddar cheese, shredded
1/2	teaspoon paprika	1	cup fresh breadcrumbs
1	teaspoon salt		

Preheat oven to 375 degrees. Butter a 2-quart baking dish. Cook the macaroni according to package directions until it is al dente (tender but not mushy). Drain. In a heavy saucepan, melt the butter over medium heat. Add the flour, stir and cook 1 minute. Whisk in the milk, paprika and salt. Bring to a boil, stirring constantly for 2 to 3 minutes until thickened. In a large bowl, stir together the cooked macaroni, 3/4 of the cheese and Worcestershire sauce. Transfer to baking dish. Mix remaining cheese and breadcrumbs. Sprinkle over the top. Bake 30 minutes. Serves 6.

Cheesy Beef Stroganoff
This recipe is a never-fail favorite for children.

1	pound ground beef	3/4	pound (12 ounces) Velveeta Pasteurized prepared Cheese, cut up
2	cups water		
3	cups (6 ounces) medium egg noodles, uncooked	1	can (10-3/4 ounces) condensed cream of mushroom soup
		1/4	teaspoon black pepper

Brown meat in a large skillet; drain. Stir in water. Bring to boil. Stir in noodles. Reduce heat to medium-low; cover. Simmer 10 minutes or until noodles are tender. Add cheese, soup and pepper. Stir until cheese is melted. Makes 4 to 6 servings.

Mormon Family Recipes

Barbecue Baked Chicken (campfire)

2 to 3	pounds chicken parts	1	medium onion, diced
1/4	cup butter	1/4	cup vinegar
1	cup packed brown sugar	1	cup catsup
1	green bell pepper, diced	1	bottle barbecue sauce

Preheat briquettes to high heat according to formula above. Place coals in a ring and set a heavy Dutch oven over them. When Dutch oven is hot, melt butter; stir brown sugar into butter. Add bell peppers and onions; sauté until softened. Add vinegar and catsup. Simmer for 10 minutes. Remove from heat. Put chicken pieces into oven and pour bottled barbecue sauce over all. Return pot to coals. Cover with lid and place hot coals evenly spaced on top of lid. Cook over constant heat about 1 hour. Uncover, baste and add a little water if needed. Recover pot and add more hot coals to raise heat. Cook another 30 minutes, checking several times and basting as necessary to keep chicken moist. Makes 4 to 6 servings.

Sweet and Sour Glazed Chicken

3	pounds chicken pieces, rinsed and patted dry	1	cup each: sugar, chicken broth and rice vinegar (or white wine vinegar)
1	cup cornstarch	1/2	cup catsup
1	tablespoon water	2	teaspoons soy sauce
2	eggs, lightly beaten	4	garlic cloves, minced
2	tablespoons salad oil		

Preheat oven to 450 degrees. Stir 2 tablespoons cornstarch with 2 tablespoons water; set aside. Dip chicken parts in egg, then in remaining cornstarch to coat lightly. Pour oil into a large shallow baking pan. Put pan into oven to heat oil. Place chicken pieces, meaty side down, on pan. Bake until light brown on bottom, about 30 minutes. Turn and bake until cooked through, another 30 minutes. Check for doneness by making a small slit near bone; if there is any redness, return to oven and cook longer.

In a saucepan, mix sugar, broth, vinegar, catsup, soy and garlic. Boil on high heat, stirring, until reduced by one-quarter. Add cornstarch-water mixture and bring to a boil, stirring until smooth and thick. Brush sauce over chicken. Continue baking, uncovered, until sauce bubbles, about 5 minutes. Makes 4 servings.

Stuffed Pork Tenderloin

1/4	cup currants	1/4	teaspoon leaf rosemary, crumbled
1/4	cup apricot jam (or fresh apricots, chopped)	1/4	teaspoon leaf sage, crumbled sprinkle of salt and pepper
1	pound boneless pork tenderloin	1	egg, lightly beaten
1	cup wheat bread crumbs		

Preheat oven to 400 degrees. Stir currants and apricots together; add a little water if needed to moisten. Cut tenderloin lengthwise down the center but not all the way through. Spread halves open. Place between two sheets of paper and pound with a heavy mallet until pork is flattened to an even 1/4-inch thickness.

Add crumbs, seasonings and egg to fruit mixture. Spread stuffing lengthwise down center of pork, leaving a little border at each end. Roll up lengthwise. Secure roll with string or toothpicks. Cook on rack in a roasting pan for about 45 minutes until meat is cooked through. Let stand a few minutes. Remove string or picks and slice thinly to serve. Makes 4 servings.

Chicken Breasts with Bacon and Cheddar Cheese Sauce

6	boneless chicken breasts (cut into 3 sections each)	1/3	cup milk dash cayenne pepper
1	tablespoon butter	1	cup fresh breadcrumbs
1	pound fresh asparagus	6	slices bacon, cooked & crumbled
1	10-ounce can condensed Cheddar cheese soup	1	cup grated Cheddar cheese

Sauté chicken breast pieces in the butter until browned and nearly cooked through. Partially cook the asparagus (it should be crispy). Arrange the asparagus in a center line in the bottom of a 9" x 13" baking dish. Place chicken on top of asparagus. In the meantime heat the soup with the milk and cayenne pepper. Pour over the chicken. Mix the crumbs and cheese and sprinkle on top of soup mixture. Top with the bacon. Bake in a preheated (350°) oven for 25-30 minutes. Serves 4-6

Lamb Kebabs

1-2	pounds lamb	Assorted vegetables;.
1	bunch fresh rosemary	onions, peppers, mushrooms
1	bunch fresh thyme	

Cut the meat into pieces that are more or less the same size, ranging from 1/2 - 1 inch on a side. As much as possible, work with the structure of the meat, discarding as much fat and sinew as you can. Thread the prepared meat onto skewers along with assorted vegetables — onion, mushrooms, and peppers. Brush the meat and vegetables with olive oil. Lay down the skewers on hot preheated grill. Turn the skewers as the meat cooks, adding the fresh herbs to the fire. The smallest pieces of meat will cook in 3 to 5 minutes, larger pieces in 8 to 10 minutes. Lamb is best when eaten rare. When done, transfer the kebabs to a platter. Season with salt and pepper. Serves 4

Glazed Ham with Pineapple
(A stored food favorite for 12)

1	boneless ham (5 to 6 pounds) fully cooked	3	cans (9 ounces each) pineapple or 12 large slices
1	cup maple flavored syrup		Spiced crab apples, optional
1	cup brown sugar		Parsley for garnish
2	tablespoons prepared mustard		

Preheat oven to 325 degrees. Have butcher cut ham into 1/2-inch thick slices. Press slices back together and secure with kitchen string. Bake on rack in roasting pan, uncovered, for 1-1/2 hours. Remove from oven. Increase heat to 400 degrees. Cut string and insert drained pineapple slices between ham slices; re-tie with string. In small saucepan, stir syrup, brown sugar and mustard to combine. Heat until blended. Brush sauce generously over ham. Return to oven 15 minutes longer, basting several times. Remove string and serve on warmed platter garnished with crab apples and parsley. Add pineapple juice to any remaining glaze; heat and serve to table. Makes 12 servings.

Meat Loaf
A traditional family favorite.

2	pounds ground meat	1/2	cup dry bread crumbs
1	small onion, finely chopped	1	teaspoon salt
1	large jar (28 ounces) chunky garden-style pasta sauce	1/4	teaspoon pepper
1	large egg, slightly beaten	1	tablespoon fresh parsley, finely chopped

Preheat over to 350 degrees. In large bowl, combine ground beef, 1 cup pasta sauce, onion, egg and bread crumbs. Season with salt and pepper. Shape meat mixture into a loaf in a baking dish. Bake uncovered 45 minutes. Pour remaining sauce over meat loaf and sprinkle with parsley. Bake an additional 15 minutes to warm sauce. Serves 6

Pork Chops with Apples

2	teaspoons vegetable oil	1	can (6 ounces) frozen unsweetened apple juice concentrate
4	pork chops, about 1 inch thick		
2	large cooking apples (McIntosh, Granny Smith)	2	teaspoons honey-mustard
			salt and pepper

Heat oil in medium-size skillet. Add chops; cook, turning occasionally, until cooked through, 8 to 10 minutes. Transfer to a warm platter. Pare, core and cut apples crosswise into rings about 1/4-inch thick. Place apple rings in skillet; cook several minutes until lightly browned. Add apple juice concentrate. Bring to a boil. Stir in mustard, salt and pepper. Serve apples and sauce over chops. Makes 4 servings.

Leg of Lamb with Mint Glaze

1	leg of lamb (4 to 5 pounds)	2	cloves garlic, crushed
1	jar (10 ounces) mint-flavored apple jelly	2	tablespoons water

Preheat oven to 325 degrees. In saucepan, heat jelly, garlic and water, stirring constantly, until jelly is melted. Place lamb on rack in a shallow roasting pan. Roast 1 hour; remove from oven, brush with jelly sauce. Return to oven; baste with additional glaze every 15 minutes. Cook 1 to 1-1/2-hours longer or until meat thermometer registers 160 degrees (for medium). Roast will carve easier if allowed to rest for 10 to 15 minutes before serving. Makes 6 servings.

Ham with Red Eye Gravy

4	slices country ham, about 1/2 inches thick	1/2	cup strong brewed coffee
2	tablespoons water	1/8	teaspoon salt

Preheat coals for high heat. Slash fat on edges of ham slices in several places. Place ham in a hot skillet; brown quickly on each side. Add water; simmer for 15 minutes or until tender. Remove from pan; keep warm. Sprinkle salt in hot skillet; add coffee. Scrap pan drippings; bring to a boil and stir for 3 minutes. Pour over ham. Serve with biscuits or grits. Makes 4 servings.

Mormon Family Recipes

FISH AND GAME

Many Mormon families depend on hunting in the fall to augment their food storage for the winter. Venison and game birds are often preferred over other meats and poultry. Mormons also eat fish frequently, although canned fish is more compatible with storage limitations.

Sautéed Trout

4	whole trout, about 3/4 pound each, gutted and split	1	cup cornmeal for coating
			salt and pepper to taste
4	tablespoons butter (or olive oil)		lemon wedges or parsley leaves for garnish

Rinse and dry fish. Melt butter in a large skillet. Dredge the fish in the cornmeal, place in pan and raise heat to high. Season with salt and pepper and cook on both sides until nicely browned and the interior turns white, 8 to 12 minutes total. Garnish with lemon wedges or parsley leaves to serve. Makes 4 servings.

Baked Fish Fillet

Lakes and streams are plentiful in Utah and game fish are abundant. This recipe will adapt to various varieties of trout, whitefish, carp, bass, perch, crappie and other mild fish.

2	pounds fish fillets	1	tablespoon grated onion
	salt and pepper	1/4	cup butter, melted
2	tablespoons lemon juice		sprinkle of paprika

Preheat oven to 350 degrees. Season fillets with salt and pepper. Mix lemon juice, onion and butter. Dip fish into butter mixture; place in a greased baking dish. Pour remaining butter over fish. Bake uncovered 30 minutes or until fish flakes easily with fork. Sprinkle with paprika. Makes 4 servings.

Roast Venison Large Cuts

(Shoulder, Tenderloin, Rump or Round) This marinade is suggested for buck deer roasts.

2	cups red wine vinegar	1	onion, chopped
4	bay leaves	2	celery sticks, chopped
20	juniper berries	2	carrots, chopped
6	cloves	1/2	cup olive oil
5	garlic cloves, lightly smashed	1/2	cup beef broth
20	peppercorns	1	venison roast (6 to 8 pounds)

Combine red wine vinegar with spices and vegetables. Gradually whisk in oil and broth until blended. Place marinade into a large resealable plastic bag (or container) that is large enough to hold the roast. Add the meat and seal bag (or cover container) so that the roast is surrounded by liquid (or plan to turn and baste meat several times). Marinate, refrigerated, for 24 to 72 hours.

Preheat oven to 400 degrees. Remove roast and dry it with paper towels. Strain liquid and discard the solids. Place meat on a rack in a roasting pan. Roast for 30 minutes, basting once with the reserved marinade. Lower the oven to 350 degrees. Continue to roast the meat, basting several times with remaining marinade and pan juices, for 1 hour, or until internal temperature (taken with meat thermometer) is 135 degrees in the thickest spot. Remove from oven and let rest before carving. Makes 8 to 10 servings.

Marinated Teriyaki Jerky

2	pounds lean meat (venison, turkey or elk)	1	teaspoon freshly grated ginger root (or 1/2 teaspoon dried ground ginger)
1/4	cup soy sauce	1	tablespoon sugar
		1	teaspoon salt

Marinade: Mix all ingredients except meat. Slice meat into 1/4-inch slices about 1 to 2 inches wide. Place meat in shallow pan in layers, brushing some marinade over each layer. Cover with plastic wrap and press meat down with another dish that will fit inside meat dish; use heavy weight to compress meat while it marinates overnight. Remove meat strips and pat dry with paper towels. Arrange in single layers on racks in shallow baking pans. (Or place foil on bottom of oven and drape meat strips over oven racks). Do not overlap pieces. Dry at 150 degrees for 8 to 10 hours until jerky cracks but does not break when bent. Pat off any excess fat on surface while jerky is warm. Cool and store in an airtight container. Refrigerate for up to 2 weeks.

Grilled Squab (or Quail)

4	squab, about 1 pound each, innards and excess fat removed, rinsed and patted dry	2	teaspoons sugar
		1/4	cup soy sauce
1	tablespoon olive oil	1	teaspoon dark sesame oil
1	teaspoon minced garlic	1/2	teaspoon freshly ground black pepper
2	tablespoons minced shallots		

Split bird at backbone and butterfly. Mix together marinade ingredients, pour over squab and marinate for up to 2 hours in the refrigerator. Preheat grill or broiler to high. Place on rack about 2 inches from heat. Grill about 6 minutes per side, basting frequently and turning once. Do not overcook. It should be crispy outside and tender inside. 4 to 6 servings.

Lamb Chops with Herbs

1/3	cup vegetable oil	1/2	teaspoon each: garlic powder, oregano, rosemary, thyme, marjoram, dry mustard and white pepper
1/3	cup red wine vinegar		
2	tablespoons soy sauce		
1	tablespoon lemon juice	8	lamb loin chops (about 2-1/2 pounds) cut 1-inch thick
1	tablespoon seasoned salt		

Combine all ingredients, except lamb; mix well. Remove 1/2 of marinade for basting. Place chops in a resealable plastic bag and pour remaining marinade over them. Seal bag and refrigerate for at least 1 hour, turning occasionally. Remove chops from marinade. Discard used marinade. Grill or broil chops until desired doneness, about 8 minutes, turning once and basting often with remaining 1/2 marinade. Discard any remaining marinade. Makes 4 to 6 servings.

"Yea, flesh also of beasts and of the fowls of the air, I, the Lord, have ordained for the use of man with thanksgiving; nevertheless they are to be used sparingly."
…..Doctrine and Covenants, Section 89, Verse 12

Herb-Marinated Flank Steak

3	tablespoons vegetable oil	1/4	teaspoon pepper
2	tablespoons red wine vinegar	2	green onions, including some of the green tops, chopped
1	teaspoon Worcestershire sauce		
1/4	teaspoon dried basil, crumbled	1	clove garlic, minced
1/4	teaspoon dried rosemary, crumbled	1	flank steak, about 2-1/2 pounds
1/2	teaspoon salt		

To make marinade, stir together all ingredients, except steak, in a small bowl. Place steak in a shallow dish (or a plastic bag) and pour marinade over the top. Cover dish (or seal bag) and refrigerate for 2 to 3 hours. Remove 30 minutes before cooking.
Preheat broiler. Remove meat from marinade. Place on an oiled broiler pan and broil, turning once, 4 to 5 minutes on each side for medium-rare. Do not overcook. To serve, cut thin slices on the diagonal and arrange on a warmed platter. Makes 6 servings.

Pioneer Stew
(An old-time stored food favorite)

1	tablespoon oil	1	can (15 ounces) kidney or pinto beans, drained
1	pound ground beef	1-1/2	teaspoon chili powder
1/2	cup onion, chopped	1	teaspoon salt
1/2	cup green bell pepper, finely diced	1	tablespoon flour combined with 2 tablespoons water
1	can (15 ounces) whole-kernel corn, drained		
1	can (15 ounces) tomatoes, undrained	1/2	cup shredded sharp Cheddar cheese

Preheat coals to high. Cook ground beef, onion and pepper in hot Dutch oven until meat is brown and vegetables are tender; drain off fat. Stir corn, tomatoes and beans into pot with chili powder. Add salt to taste. Simmer 30 minutes. Separately, combine flour with 2 tablespoons water. Stir into stew; cover and cook over medium heat another 30 minutes, stirring occasionally. Serve with cheese sprinkled over top. Serves 6 to 8.

Pepper Steak

1 teaspoon each: black, white and green dried peppercorns or 1 tablespoon dried black peppercorns	1/2 cup finely chopped shallot or white part of green onion
1 boneless sirloin steak about 1-1/2 inches thick, (about 2 pounds)	1 tablespoon flour
	1 cup beef broth
	1/4 teaspoon Worcestershire sauce
1 tablespoon vegetable oil	2 tablespoons fresh parsley, finely chopped
2 tablespoons unsalted butter	Salt to taste

Crush peppercorns in plastic bag with a rolling pin or meat hammer. Rub onto both sides of steak. Let steak marinate for at least 30 minutes. If longer, refrigerate. Heat oil in large, heavy skillet (or cast iron Dutch oven) over moderately high heat. Add steak; cook 5 to 7 minutes each side for rare. Transfer to platter to keep warm.

Pour off fat from skillet. Add 1 tablespoon butter and shallot to skillet; cook over moderate heat, stirring, for 2 minutes. Stir in flour; cook, stirring, for 1 minute. Slowly add beef broth. Bring to boiling; lower heat, simmer 3 minutes. Stir in remaining 1 tablespoon butter and parsley. Salt steak if desired. Pour sauce over steak. Makes 6 servings.

One-Dish Mexican Skillet

1 tablespoon oil	1 can (15-ounces) kidney or pinto beans, drained
1 pound ground beef	Salt and chili powder, to taste
1/2 cup chopped onion	
1 can (10-3/4 ounces) tomato soup	1 box cornbread mix
1 soup can water	

Preheat coals to high heat. Brown ground beef and onion in oil in cast iron skillet. Add soup, water, beans and seasonings. Mix cornbread according to directions and pour on top of meat mixture. Cover skillet; place coals on top to maintain 350 degrees. Bake about 20 to 30 minutes. Makes 4 servings.

Mormon Family Recipes

CAST IRON COOKING

For centuries, cast iron cookware has been passed-down from generation to generation and has been used on the open hearth, the open trail and the stove top. One of the most versatile of these pots is the Dutch oven, a heavy pot, usually 10 to 20-inches diameter, with a tightly-fitted lid. The pots designed for outdoor cooking have short legs and a rimmed lid so that coals may be placed under the pot and on top of the lid. Heat from the bottom and top of the pot create a cooking condition similar to a conventional oven in which food may be baked, braised or roasted. A Dutch oven is an important utensil for family preparedness and self-reliance. Any recipe that can be cooked in a skillet on top the stove, or in a roasting pan or baking dish inside the oven may be cooked in the Dutch oven over hot coals outdoors.

NUMBER OF CHARCOALS NEEDED FOR DUTCH OVEN COOKING

Most Dutch ovens are 10 to 16-inches in diameter. Follow this formula for the number of coals and place 1/3 of the coals under the Dutch oven and 2/3 of the coals on the lid.

FOR MODERATE HEAT: The diameter of the Dutch oven multiplied by 2 equals the number of coals to use; i.e. 12-inch pot x 2 equals 24 coals. Place 1/3 (or 8 coals) under the pot and 2/3 (or 16 coals) on the lid.

FOR HIGH HEAT: The diameter of the Dutch oven multiplied by 3 equals the total number of coals needed. For a 12-inch pot, use 36 coals. Place 12 coals under the pot and 24 coals on the lid.

FOR MAINTAINING HEAT OVER AN HOUR: To maintain heat for more that an hour, ignite 10 to 12 extra coals and add 4 to 5 coals after each 20 or 30 minutes of cooking.

A sampling of outdoor-cast-iron-cooking recipes although almost any foods will adapt to these cooking techniques.

Whole Wheat Bread
(A basic food storage favorite)

1	package active dry yeast
1/2	cup warm water (110 to 115 degrees)
1	cup milk
1/2	cup boiling water
1/4	cup sugar or molasses
2	teaspoons salt
4	cups all-purpose flour
2	cups whole wheat flour
	shortening

Combine yeast and water in mixing bowl, let stand 5 minutes. In a separate bowl, stir milk, boiling water, sugar (or molasses) and salt. Mix well; cool to lukewarm and add to the yeast mixture. Stir in flour, a cup at a time, until dough is formed. Turn out on a lightly floured board and knead about 10 minutes or until smooth and satiny. Place dough in a warm, greased bowl; brush surface with melted shortening. Cover and let rise in a warm place (80 to 85 degrees) until doubled in size, about 1 hour. Shape into 2 loaves. Place in greased loaf pans and let rise again to almost double in size, about 1 hour. Bake in a hot oven (400 degrees) for abut 45 minutes. Makes 2 loaves.

Cornbread

1-1/2	cups yellow cornmeal		3/4	cup unsalted butter, melted and cooled
1	cup all-purpose flour, sifted		2	large eggs, lightly beaten
1	tablespoon baking powder		1-1/2	cups milk
1-1/4	teaspoon salt			

Preheat oven to 375 degrees. Butter a 9-inch square pan. In a mixing bowl, sift together the cornmeal, flour, baking powder and salt. Add butter, eggs and milk; stir until combined. Pour into pan and bake 40 minutes. Makes 6 servings.

"All grain is ordained for the use of man and of beasts, to be the staff of life…"
…..Doctrine and Covenants, Section 89, Verse 14

Best Basic White Bread

2	packages active dry yeast	2	tablespoons sugar
2	cups warm water	1	tablespoon salt
	(110 to 115 degrees)	1/3	cup cooking oil
1/2	cup nonfat dry milk		7 to 7-1/2 cups flour

Sprinkle yeast into warm water. Stir to dissolve. Add dry milk, sugar, salt, oil and 3 cups flour. Beat with electric mixer at medium speed until smooth, about 3 minutes, scraping bowl occasionally. Add enough remaining flour, a little at a time, to make a dough that leaves the sides of the bowl. Turn on lightly-floured board, cover and leave to rest for 10 minutes. Knead until smooth and elastic, about 10 minutes. Divide dough into half; shape each half into a loaf. Place in two greased 9x5x3 inch loaf pans. Let rise until doubled, about 1 hour. Bake in 400 degree oven for 30 minutes or until tops are golden brown and loaf sounds hollow when tapped. Cool on wire racks. Makes 2 loaves.

Mormon Muffins

Recipe courtesy of the Greenery Restaurant, Ogden, Utah

2	cups boiling water	5	cups flour
5	teaspoons baking soda	1	teaspoon salt
1	cup shortening	4	cups All Bran Cereal
2	cups sugar	2	cups 40% Bran Flakes
4	eggs	1	cup walnuts, chopped
1	quart buttermilk		

The Greenery Restaurant recommends that the mix be made a day ahead and be refrigerated overnight. Preheat oven to 350 degrees when ready to bake.

Premix: Add soda to boiling water and set aside. Whip shortening and sugar until light and fluffy. Add the eggs one at a time, mixing well with each addition. Add buttermilk, flour and salt. Mix thoroughly. Add the soda water very slowly. Gently fold in the cereals and walnuts. Spoon 1/4 cup into greased muffin tins. Bake at 350 degrees for 30 minutes. Cool for 5 minutes. Yields 3 dozen muffins.

Boston Brown Quick Bread

This is the traditional accompaniment to baked beans.

1	cup rye flour	1	teaspoon salt
1	cup yellow cornmeal	3/4	cup molasses
1	cup white flour	2	cups buttermilk
2	teaspoons baking soda		

Mix dry ingredients; stir in molasses and buttermilk, mixing well, but do not beat. Fill 1-1/2 quart mold two-thirds full. Cover with tight-fitting lid or aluminum foil. Place on a rack in a tightly-covered Dutch oven or stock pot; containing a small amount of boiling water. Steam 2 to 3-1/2 hours, or until wooden pick inserted in center comes out clean. Keep water boiling over low heat throughout cooking, adding more water as needed. (To add, boil water in another container, lift lid and quickly add water so that the least possible amount of steam is lost). Remove from mold and serve hot with butter (or remove and wrap in waxed paper and return to mold to reheat later). Makes enough for one 7-inch tube mold or four 1-pound cans. Serves 8 to 10.

Canned Fruit Cobbler
(A stored food favorite)

3	cups fruit (canned or fresh, sliced as if for pie)	1-1/2	teaspoon baking powder
		1/2	teaspoon salt
3	tablespoons butter	1/3	cup vegetable oil
1	cup sugar	3	tablespoons milk
1/2	teaspoon cinnamon	1	egg, slightly beaten
1	cup flour, divided		

Preheat oven to 350 degrees. Prepare fruit and arrange on the bottom of a greased 8x8-inch baking pan or a 10-inch Dutch oven. Cut butter into sugar, cinnamon and 2 tablespoons flour until it resembles fine crumbs. Sprinkle over fruit. Combine remaining dry ingredients. Make a well in the flour mixture and stir in oil, milk and egg. Blend with a fork until moistened. Spoon by tablespoons over top of fruit. Bake for 25 to 30 minutes. Serves 6 to 8.

Quick Apple Crisp

8	Granny Smith apples, sliced	1	cup flour
3	tablespoons sugar	2	teaspoons cinnamon
1-1/2	cups quick oats	1/4	teaspoon nutmeg
1-1/2	cups brown sugar	3/4	cup butter

Preheat oven to 350 degrees. Arrange apple slices in a greased, deep baking dish. Sprinkle sugar over slices. Combine oats, brown sugar, flour and spices. Cut in butter. Mix well and spread over apples. Bake for 35 to 40 minutes. Serve warm with cheese, whipped cream or ice cream. Makes 6 to 8 servings.

Breads & Desserts

Pumpkin Pie

3/4	cup sugar	2	eggs
1/2	teaspoon salt	1	can (15 ounces) pumpkin (not pie mix)
1	teaspoon cinnamon	1	can evaporated milk
1/2	teaspoon ground ginger	1	unbaked 9-inch deep dish pie shell
1/4	teaspoon ground cloves		whipped cream

Preheat oven to 425 degrees then reduce heat to 350 degrees when ready to bake. Mix sugar and spices in a small bowl. Beat eggs in a larger mixing bowl. Stir in pumpkin and sugar/spice mixture. Gradually stir in evaporated milk. Pour into pie shell. Bake 40 to 50 minutes or until knife inserted near center comes out clean. Cool on wire rack. Serve with whipped cream, if desired. Makes 8 servings.

Apple Crisp Dutch-Oven Dessert

3/4	cup butter (1-1/2 sticks)	1	cup flour
8	tart apples, such as Granny Smith	2	teaspoons cinnamon
1-1/2	cups quick oats	1.4	teaspoon nutmeg
1-1/2	cups brown sugar		

Prepare Dutch oven to cook at moderate heat. Melt butter in bottom of pot. Peel, core and slice apples into a mixing bowl. Add the remaining ingredients and stir together with the butter in the Dutch oven. Cover and bake for 45 minutes. Serves 6 to 8.

Sugar Cookies

1	cup butter	2-1/2	cups all-purpose flour
1-1/2	cups confectioners powdered sugar	1	teaspoon baking soda
1	egg	1	teaspoon cream of tartar
1	teaspoon vanilla		granulated sugar
1/2	teaspoon almond extract		

Combine butter, powdered sugar, egg, vanilla and almond extract. Blend in flour, soda and cream of tartar. Cover; chill several hours. Preheat oven to 375 degrees. Divide dough in half. Roll each half 3/16-inch thick on lightly floured board. Cut into desired shapes; sprinkle with granulated sugar. Bake on lightly greased baking sheet for 7 to 8 minutes or until light brown around the edge. Makes about 4 dozen three-inch cookies.

Strawberry Shortcake

Blueberries, blackberries or raspberries may also be used in this recipe.

2	cups all-purpose flour	3/4	cup shortening
2	tablespoons sugar	1	cup milk
1	tablespoon baking powder	3	cups fresh strawberries
1	teaspoon salt		whipped topping (optional)

Preheat oven to 450 degrees. Combine flour, sugar, baking powder and salt. Cut shortening into flour mixture until mixture resembles coarse cornmeal. Blend in milk; mix well. Spread dough in a 9x9-inch baking pan. Bake 15 minutes. Serve warm or let cool. Top with strawberries before serving. Garnish with whipped topping, if desired. Makes 6 to 8 servings.

Breads & Desserts

Vanilla Coffee-Can Ice Cream

(A fun-Friday-night favorite)

1	cup heavy cream	1/2	cup sugar
1	cup light cream	1	teaspoon vanilla extract
1	egg, beaten		

Combine all ingredients and place in a 1-pound coffee can. Seal the lid well with duct tape. Put the small, sealed can inside a larger 3-pound can. Pack ice and 1 cup rock salt around small can. Place lid on large can and seal well with duct tape. Roll back and forth on a large towel for 15 minutes. Open large can and discard ice and water. Wipe small can dry. Open and stir ice cream, scraping sides. Additional ingredients, such as cookie crumbs, sprinkles or nuts, can be added now. Reseal small can and place back in larger can. Repack with salt and ice. Continue rolling for 10 or 15 minutes more. Open large can and discard ice and water. Wipe small can dry and serve ice cream. Makes 4 servings.

Chocolate Ice Cream

Same recipe as Vanilla, except add 4 tablespoons cocoa to sugar then proceed as directed.

Doughnuts

3	cups flour
1	cup sugar
1/2	cup milk
1	egg
1	teaspoon butter
1	teaspoon soda
2	teaspoon baking powder
1/2	teaspoon vanilla or nutmeg

Mix all ingredients together. Roll the dough out to ½ inch thickness and cut in doughnut shapes. Fill a medium heavy pot about half full of cooking oil and heat to 360°. When oil is hot, drop doughnuts and fry a few at a time until light brown turning once to brown both sides. Makes 24

Baked Apples in Pastry

6	apples	10	tablespoons ice-cold water
3	cups flour	1/2	cup butter
1 1/2	teaspoons salt	1/2	cup sugar
3/4	cup cold vegetable shortening	1	teaspoon combination of cinnamon, cloves and nutmeg
1/2	cup Cheddar cheese		
1/2	cup ground or chopped walnuts		

Sift flour and salt into a medium-size bowl; cut in shortening until crumbly; stir in cheese & walnuts. Sprinkle water over mixture; mix lightly with fork until pastry holds together and leaves the sides of the bowl. Remove from bowl; knead into a smooth ball (add more flour if necessary); set aside. Pare apples and core just to the bottom, leaving bottom intact. Remove any seeds. Combine butter, sugar, and spices in a small bowl until smooth and paste-like. Spoon into centers of apples. Roll out the pastry; cut into 7-inch squares. Place pastry square on top of apple and press pastry firmly around apple, sealing at the bottom. Add pastry "leaves" & "stems" if desired. Place in a lightly greased baking sheet and bake at 425º F for 45 minutes. Serve warm. Serves 6

Missionaries' Scotch Shortbread

This is a favorite treat that mothers send to children on missions.

| 2 | cups butter | 4 | cups flour |
| 1 | cup confectioners powdered sugar | 1/3 | cup cornstarch |

Cream butter; gradually add sugar. Beat until light. Sift flour and cornstarch together. Add to butter mixture, a little at a time, until all flour has been blended. Knead the dough on a lightly floured board for 5 minutes. Use a rolling pin to roll to 1/2-inch thickness. Cut into 1-1/2 inch squares. Prick the tops of each with fork tines. Bake on an ungreased cookie sheet for 25 to 30 minutes or until lightly browned. Remove shortbread to rack to cool. Shortbread will keep indefinitely stored in a foil-lined tin with a tight lid. Makes 5 dozen squares.

Rice Pudding

3	cups milk	1	cup raisins
1/2	cup sugar	2-3	tablespoons butter
2	cups cooked rice	1	teaspoon vanilla extract

Combine milk, sugar, rice, raisins and butter in saucepan. Simmer for 20 to 30 minutes until thick. Remove from heat and stir in vanilla. Serves 4 to 6.